THE CRICKETER'S QUOTATION BOOK

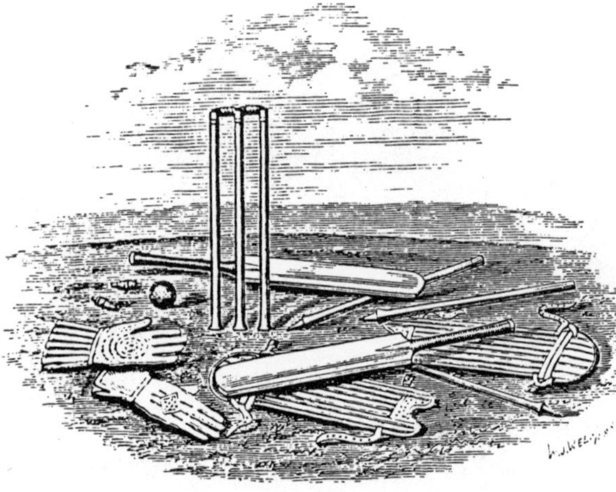

The Cricketer's Quotation Book

A Literary Companion

Edited by
DAVID RAYVERN ALLEN

ROBERT HALE · LONDON

Preface and selection © David Rayvern Allen 1995
First published in Great Britain 1995

ISBN 0 7090 5325 8

Robert Hale Limited
Clerkenwell House
Clerkenwell Green
London EC1R 0HT

The right of David Rayvern Allen to be identified
as author of this work has been asserted by him
in accordance with the Copyright, Designs
and Patents Act 1988.

2 4 6 8 10 9 7 5 3 1

Photoset in Goudy by
Derek Doyle & Associates, Mold, Clwyd.
Printed in Great Britain by
St Edmundsbury Press, Bury St Edmunds, Suffolk.
Bound by WBC Book Manufacturers Ltd.,
Bridgend, Mid-Glamorgan.

Acknowledgements

The editor would like to thank the following authors, agents and publishers for permission to use quotations: *Cricket*, by C.L.R. James, edited by Anna Grimshaw (Allison and Busby, London); *The Lyttelton–Hart-Davis Letters*, Rupert Hart-Davis, (John Murray (Publishers) Ltd); *Summer Days*, Michael Meyer (Eyre Methuen Ltd); Beryl Bainbridge; Melvyn Bragg; Richard Scott Simon Ltd; Jacky Gillot, Peters, Fraser and Dunlop; Michael Holroyd, A.P. Watt Ltd; P.J. Cavanagh; Sir Bernard Lovell; Reed Consumer Books.

Every effort has been made to trace copyright holders but the publishers offer their apologies where this has proved impossible.

Preface

Somebody is supposed to have said, 'those who can't play cricket write about it', and if they did not they ought to have done. Fortunately, a number of these would-be players were literary lions who settled for strokes on the printed page.

One difficulty with a book of cricket quotations is not what to put in, but what not to put in: to choose is to exclude, unavoidably. The game has been part of the social fabric for so long that practically everybody who was a somebody – it is not an exclusive qualification – seems to have had a view.

Many of those views are in a room without one. My study, for want of a grandiose term, is little more than a book depository – a depository majorly full of books on cricket. If you tread carefully, you can find a lot of what has been said about the game – eventually. You will also find books that are not on cricket, ostensibly, but search within and, more often than not, there is a hidden gem. An allusion to cricket is just as likely to be found in an obscure treatise on comparative religions as a Boys' Own Annual, and a Rastafarian handsheet.

The extraordinary thing about this exercise with bat and ball, is that it became the great metaphor for life, a yardstick for certain standards and behaviour. In fact, uniquely, it was no longer just a game. The Proust of pastimes was, according to James Barrie, an idea of the

Gods. The playright, Harold Pinter, is more particular:

I tend to believe that cricket is the greatest thing that God ever created on earth ... certainly greater than sex, although sex isn't too bad either. But everyone knows which comes first when it's a question of cricket or sex.

Naturally.

Cricket is, of course, the Englishman's birthright, or, at any rate, one of his birthrights. It should not, however, be assumed that the game was unknown to the Ancient World. There is plenty of (unreliable) evidence to show that Julius Caesar said: 'Dico, vetus puer, haec non est cicada' ('I say, old boy, this isn't cricket') to Brutus when the latter was cutting him. Be that as it may, cricket has been played pretty solidly in this country, and indeed throughout the Empire ever since the Norman Conquest, except perhaps during the Dark Ages, when bad light stopped play.
>   RALPH WOTHERSPOON AND L.N. JACKSON
>   *Some Sports and Pastimes of the English,* 1937

Quoits, Cricket, Nine-Pins and Trap Ball will be very much in fashion and more Tradesmen may be seen Playing in the Fields than working in their Shops.
>   EDWARD WARD
>   *The world bewitched: a dialogue between two astrologers (George Parker and John Partridge) and the author. With infallible predictions of what will happen in the present year,* 1699

The Cricketer's Quotation Book

According to my promis have sent you one piece of nankeen and a few peares wich I hope will com safe to hand. Last Munday youre father was at Mr Payne and plaid at cricket and came home please anuf for he struck the best ball on the game and wished he had not annything else to do he could play at cricket all his life …
>MARY TURNER
>letter from Mary Turner at East Hoathly to her son Phillip at Brighthelmstone, 1739

Sometimes an unlucky boy will drive his cricket ball full in my face.
>DR SAMUEL JOHNSON
>*The Rambler*, 1750

>While batting once, The Prince of Wales – whose name was Frederick Louis,
>Was hit upon the head, and so his legs went soft and gooey.
>He later died because he got that bouncer to the brain,
>So in his case you might say the result was 'play stopped reign'.
>>RICHARD STILGOE
>>from a song: 'The Prince of Wales'

The Cricketer's Quotation Book

Never was such a player, so safe, so brilliant, so quick, so circumspect, so able to counsel, so active in the field; in deliberation so judicious, in execution so tremendous. It mattered not to him who bowled, or how he bowled, fast or slow, high or low, straight or bias, away flew the ball from his bat like an eagle on the wing. It was a study for Phidias to see Beldham rise to strike – the grandeur of the attitude, the settled composure of the look, the piercing lightning of the eye, the rapid glance of the bat, were electrical. Men's hearts throbbed within them, their cheeks turned pale and red. Michael Angelo should have painted him. Beldham was great in every hit, but his peculiar glory was the cut. Here he stood with no man beside him, the laurel was all his own; it was like the cut of a racket. His wrist seemed to turn on springs of the finest steel. He took the ball as Burke did the House of Commons, between wind and water; not a moment too soon or too late.
    THE REVD JOHN MITFORD
    The Gentleman's Magazine, 1833

Hambledon is a place that I have a strong dislike to – on account of its morals and dissipation.
    GILBERT WHITE
    letter to his brother Revd John White, 1774
    on Hambledon, which at that time was one of
    the centres of cricket.

After the 1776 Revolution the question of a name for the Chief Executive of the USA was discussed. It was suggested that the word President be used. John Adams thereupon remarked, 'There are Presidents of fire companies and cricket clubs'.
STEPHEN GREEN
'Some Cricket Records', *Archives*, vol. XVIII, no. 80, 1988

The Cricketer's Quotation Book

AN EARLY ACCOUNT OF A CRICKET MATCH

THE CRICKET MATCH

'Tis early Spring, the lucid air
and smiling Skies make all things fair:
green Nature bids our feet, with speed,
disport them on the level mead.
I see a chosen company,
with curving bats armed gallantly,
(smoothed by deft hands for use) – and "lo!"
with shouts into the field they go.
Each boasts his own peculiar grace,
this skims the ground, supreme in pace,
hawk-eyes the moment's need to spy,
and to and fro unerring fly.
That best can hurl the ball afar
and bursts the wind's opposing bar;
that other fears no rival's skill,
when, o'er the even turf, his will
sends forth a poisèd sphere, too fleet
to reck the batsman's answering beat.
The friendly foe's loud-voiced array
greets their approach, then comes delay,
then quarrels rife, while all exclaim
and all would lord it o'er the game.
Now some grey veteran intercedes,
and wins their love, the while he pleads:
a Daniel come to judgement, he
to all around speaks equity.

The Cricketer's Quotation Book

Though now his arms be laid aside,
and marred by years his early pride,
yet rich is he in cricket lore,
and proves that they need strive no more.

The Lists are set where, (happy chance!)
the meadow yields a smooth expanse;
opposed, on either hand, appear
twin rods that forkèd heads uprear,
with ends set firmly in the green,
(nor wide the middle space between),
and next a milk-white Bail is laid
from fork to fork, whereby is swayed
the dubious issue of the fight,
and all must guard it with their might.
The Leathern Orb speeds forth like fate,
and should its destined line be straight
and raze the bail's support, defeat
ensues and sorrowful retreat.
Each at his wicket, near at hand,
propped on his staff, the Umpires stand,
the runner's bat must touch their pale,
or else the run will nought avail.

On a low mound, whence clear the view,
repose a trusty pair and true:
their simple task, with ready blade,
notches to cut, as runs are made.
The Players now ranged out at length,
two sides are picked, of equal strength.

The Cricketer's Quotation Book

a Coin goes up, now, Fortune, say,
who first shall bat, or we, or they!
Ere yet the brave encounter start,
each youth stands ready for his part.
Yet graver cares must him befall,
whose office is to bowl the ball,
then stop its sharp return, and hold
it fast, by either hand controlled.
While others to their work he sends,
how busy he to gain his ends!
Around him spreads the brisk array,
and waits the word that heralds 'Play.'

The Issue's joined, two chiefs of name
go forth, both heroes of the game.
The word is given, and, urged with might,
speeds the greased ball in level flight,
and o'er the grassy surface sweeps;
with bended knee the batsman keeps
a forward stance, to watch its way
and mark it rise, then *sans* delay.
His arms descend with lightning fall,
to smite amain the ringing ball;
and, ringing on, sublime it flies
and disappears into the Skies.

Meanwhile some wary Scout afield
brings craft to make the victor yield,
views the descent with upward eyes,
till his stretched hands secure the prize;

then gaily throws it up once more,
cheered by his friends' exultant roar.
But silent bows the foeman's head,
in anguish for a comrade sped.
Woe worth the day! Yet, eager still,
another comes the breach to fill.
Fired with high hopes, his noble heat
essays to overwhelm defeat.
Yet Fortune frowns, the bowler's force
four times accomplishes the course,
and thrice the batsman plays his part.
Then, headlong flung with desperate art,
the ball prevents the bat, and shears
the light bail rudely from its piers.
The Victim, reddening with dismay,
shoulders his bat and walks away,
mourning his luck and low estate,
until the coming of his mate.
He, to a sinking banner true,
renews a fray he soon shall rue.
Anon, between the wickets pent,
on runs this way and that intent,
he slips, he falls, unhappy soul!
Upon the threshold of his goal,
flat on the earth, with sounding thwack,
while jeers aloud the rustic pack.
To each his innings: and its end,
that comes too soon our case to mend;
for, be it *Fate*, or lack of *Skill*,
our efforts are but failures still;

back flows the current of success,
as downcast looks and moods confess.
'Neath happier stars, the aspiring foe
distress the ball with blow on blow:
hot is the pace, each brow bedewed,
with linkèd triumphs oft renewed
waxes the strife, but one notch more,
and mastery will crown the score.
'Tis done! the stricken sphere ascends
heavenward, on airs the South Wind lends:
and, ended now the long debate,
Dame Victory claps her wings, elate,
and makes the Sky with cheers articulate.
   WILLIAM GOLDWIN
  'In Certamen Pilae', 1706
  translated Harold Perry, 1922

What is human life but a game of cricket? and if so, why should not the ladies play it as well as we?

Methinks I heard some little macaroni youth, some trifling apology for the figure of a man, exclaiming with the greatest vehemence. How can the ladies hurt their delicate hands, and even bring them to blisters, with holding a nasty filthy bat? How can their sweet delicate fingers bear the jarrings attending the catching of a dirty ball?

Mind not, my dear ladies, the impertinent interrogatories of silly cox-combs, or the dreadful apprehensions of demi-men. Let your sex go on and assert their right to every pursuit that does not debase the mind. Go on, and attach yourselves to the athletic, and by that convince your neighbours the French that you despise their washes, their paint and their pomatons, and that you are now determined to convince all Europe how worthy you are of being considered the wives of plain, generous, and native Englishmen!

THE 3RD DUKE OF DORSET
Ladies & Gentlemen's Magazine, 1777

Female Cricketers. Eleven women of Lyndhurst and Minstead played other eleven of Poulner and Picket Post on Thursday, when the latter were victorious. The scene was a disgusting one and altogether discreditable to the district.

CUTTING FROM A RINGWOOD NEWSPAPER, 1850

I only ever played the game once myself, in the park with some evacuees from Bootle. I was allowed to join in because I held a biscuit tin filled with shortbread that my mother had baked. They said I could have a turn if I gave them a biscuit afterwards. I didn't make any runs because I never hit the ball, and when I kept my promise and began to open the tin the evacuees knocked me over and took every piece of shortbread. They threw the tin over the wall into the gentlemen's lavatory. I had to tell my mother a six-foot-high naughty man with a Hitler moustache had chased me; she would have slapped me for playing with evacuees.

BERYL BAINBRIDGE
The Longstop, 1981

The Cricketer's Quotation Book

I longed for the dramatic catch, for the Angela Brazil moment of running, judging, squinting, reaching and then rolling to the ground, that crimson treasure clasped triumphantly to the ribcage. I practised the movements with an imaginary ball in my bedroom. But no other girl, it seemed, shared this vision. Some hapless creature, having done a careful manicure during break and seeing the ball drop towards her from the sky, would raise both arms more in supplication than determination, then let it plop between her arms preferring to be damned than break her nicely fashioned nails. Some didn't even have the decency to pretend the sun had dazzled them. They just grinned cheerfully and went back to the business of acquiring a tan.
    JACKY GILLOT
    Twelfth Man, 1981

Although we have all on occasions enjoyed proper muscular exercise, yet we strongly reprobate that of cricket, which is in all respects too violent, and, from the positions into which players must necessarily throw themselves, cannot fail to be productive of frequent injury to the body. Indeed, we have witnessed several melancholy accidents which lately happened in our neighbourhood; from the awkward posture occasioned by employing both arms at the same time in striking a distant object.
    Dr. Willich's Domestic Encyclopaedia, 1802

The Cricketer's Quotation Book

We have played the Eton and were most confoundedly beat, however it was some comfort to me that I got eleven notches in the first innings and seven the second …
>LORD BYRON
>>letter referring to initial match in series in 1805.
>>Byron's actual scores were somewhat different

In short, we were a nest of singing-birds. Here we walked, here we played at cricket.
>DR SAMUEL JOHNSON
>>reply to Hannah More who, during a tour of his
>>old College, Pembroke, in 1782, had pointed
>>out all the rooms of the poets
>>Hannah More, *Memoirs*, 1834

That Bill's a foolish fellow;
He has given me a black eye.
He does not know how to handle a bat
Any more than a dog, or a cat;
He has knock'd down the wicket,
And broken his stumps
And runs without shoes to save his pumps.
>WILLIAM BLAKE
>>'The Song of Tilly Lally'

Capital gain – smart sport – fine exercise – very.
>JINGLE
>>in Charles Dickens' *Pickwick Papers*, 1836

The Cricketer's Quotation Book

Personally, I have always looked on cricket as organised loafing.
>WILLIAM TEMPLE, ARCHBISHOP OF CANTERBURY
>*Printed Sermons*

Cricket – it's more than a game. It's an institution.
>THOMAS HUGHES
>*Tom Brown's Schooldays*, 1857

The national game of England is cricket, than which none more noble, more manly, or more social exists; a game of which we Britons alone have a just right to claim the supremacy – one, in fact, which no other nation under heaven has the pluck to play; a game utterly devoid of all that is mean, cankering, or vile; a game in which princes and artizans, clergy and laity, dons and freshmen, officers and privates, scholars and clodhoppers, Anti-Teapots and Teapots, the staunch High Churchman and the 'conscientious' Dissenter, may contend in honourable rivalry; a game within the reach of all classes, dispensing with the ordinary ranks of society, not however after the manner of Mr Bright and other rank reformers, but precedence of birth, rank, and fortune, give place to superiority of skill; a game refreshing the body, relaxing, yet employing, the mind, and irresistibly driving dull care away; a game which even Teapots, ever renowned with an ill-sounding fame for crying down and fulminating against innocent amusements, allow to be worthy of their panegyrics; it is a game, in fine, widely different from, and far superior to, any other pastime. For its successful cultivation physical activity is not the only requisite, but with this must be blended intellectual and moral acquirements. Unlike rowing, it demands not of its devotees that severe training of body which has proved injurious to the health of many who have not been gifted with iron consititutions; still a moderate amount of training, not of body only, but also of the intellectual faculties, is indispensable to those whose ambition it is to enjoy a reputation in their University, college, county, town, or village.

The moral qualifications of a cricketer must be regarded as an important argument in favour of the noble game. The Russian soldiers are said to fight with greater courage when under the influence of an inebriating liquor; happily this cannot be said of the English cricketer. Drunken and debauched habits will

bring his career to a rapid and untimely close; in short, temperance, both in eating and drinking, is essential for his well-being and well-doing.
'THE PHILOSOPHY OF CRICKET'
Anti-Teapot Review, 1866

As every soldier has the bâton of a Field-Marshal in his knapsack, so every player has the bat of Lillywhite in his portmanteau.
ALMANACK, 1868

> There's a breathless hush in the Close tonight,
> Ten to make and the match to win.
> A bumping pitch and a blinding light,
> An hour to play and the last man in,
> And it's not for the sake of a ribboned coat,
> Or the selfish hope of a season's fame,
> But his Captain's hand on his shoulder smote,
> 'Play up! play up! and play the game!'
>
> The sand of the desert is sodden red, –
> Red with the wreck of a square that broke; –
> The Gatling's jammed and the Colonel dead,
> And the Regiment blind with dust and smoke.
> The river of death has brimmed his banks,
> And England's far and Honour a name,
> But the voice of a schoolboy rallies the ranks;
> 'Play up! play up! and play the game!'

The Cricketer's Quotation Book

This is the word that year by year,
While in her place the School is set,
Every one of her sons must hear,
And none that hears it dare forget.
This they all with a joyful mind
Bear through life like a torch in flame,
And falling fling to the host behind –
'Play up! play up! and play the game!'
SIR HENRY NEWBOLT
Vitaï Lampada
Admirals All and Other Verses, 1897

A distracted mother of twins suspected that they had measles. W.G.'s advice was: 'Put 'em in bed together and don't bother me unless they get up to 208 for two before lunch.'
W.G. GRACE

William Hemingway was often to be found in the dressing-room with his back to the window reading Greek. When Hemingway on one occasion complained to W.G. about his own temporary lack of success, the Old Man replied: 'How can you expect to make runs when you are always reading? I am never caught that way.'
W.G. GRACE TO WILLIAM HEMINGWAY

The Cricketer's Quotation Book

THE ENGLISH CRICKETERS TRIP TO CANADA AND THE UNITED STATES BY FRED LILLYWHITE.

The Cricketer's Quotation Book

'Mr Chairman and Gentleman, far be it from me to say that Dr Grace is stout; but his form is, let us say, manly. You will remember that the Queen of the Fairies in *Iolanthe*, a lady of noble proportions, remarked that she saw no objection to stoutness in moderation; yet, in men at least, stoutness (like the American judge) is always an object of contempt. In an athlete especially, obesity provokes derision. During the late football season a very competent goalkeeper was unkindly desired by the crowd, merely on account of his waist dimension, to go home and play with his grandchildren. In some sports Falstaff's failing would be a fatal objection: a corpulent coxswain is an impossibility. It says much for the gentle art of cricket that stoutness, if a disadvantage, is not an absolute disqualification.

E.B.W. CHRISTIAN
Coupled with the Name of W.G., 1896

Well done, Leviathan! We send thee here
A birthday greeting for thy jubilee;
Unparalleled in scoring, now this year
Another half hundred brings to thee.
Straight as thy bat has been thy course in life
And still they force unwasted forward plays;
Thy splendid vigour with decay holds strife,
And Time, that runs out all, with thee delays;
Thy fame has spread wherever bat and ball
Ring with their joyous clatter o'er the field.

The Cricketer's Quotation Book

On this thy birthday may no shadow fall
And may it still a further hundred yield;
Thou art the centre of a million eyes
Who love one summer game and sunny skies.
  'TO W.G. GRACE'
  to commemorate Grace's jubilee, 1898

G.K. Chesterton once said that Pickwick was the true English fairy, and W.G., that bulky sprite, was a prodigious Puck in a truly mid-summer's day dream.
  G.K. CHESTERTON

Had Grace been born in ancient Greece the *Iliad* would have been a different book. Had he lived in the Middle Ages, he would have been a Crusader and would now have been lying with his legs crossed in some ancient abbey, having founded a great family.
THE BISHOP OF HEREFORD
quoted by Clifford Bax in *W. G. Grace, Cricketing Lives*, 1952

The Cricketer's Quotation Book

Very few cricketers before W.G. ever attained the honour of a personal appearance in *Punch*. Jackson did. Imagine the dialogue appended to the picture of a gentleman returning from the wicket, muffled from top to toe in bandages, as from the wars.

'Good match, old fellow?'

'Oh yes; awfully jolly.'

'What did you do?'

'I had a hover of Jackson; first ball 'it me on the 'and; the second 'ad me on the knee; the third was in my eye; and the fourth bowled me out!'

    A.A. THOMSON
    Odd Men In, 1958

Go to Lord's and analyse the crowd. There are all sorts and conditions of men there round the ropes – bricklayers, bank clerks, soldiers, postmen, and stockbrokers. And in the pavilion are Q.C.s, artists, archdeacons and leader-writers. Bad men, good men, workers and idlers, are all there, and all at one in their keenness over the game ... cricket brings the most opposite characters and the most diverse lives together. Anything that puts very many different kinds of people on a common ground must promote sympathy and kindly feelings.
KUMAR RANJITSINHJI

Albert Trott, the great Middlesex, Australia and England all-rounder, bowled far too well at his own benefit match. Having destroyed Somerset with his medium-pace off-breaks the game finished early, thereby losing a great deal of potential gate-money. Lamented Trott: 'I've bowled myself into the workhouse.'
    ALBERT TROTT

Mr J.M. Barrie, the Scotch novelist – who is an ardent cricketer and when playing for the Authors against the Press at Lord's is said to have fielded 'brilliantly with his hands in his pockets' – tells a story of a man notable for his pedantry who was batting one day when Mr Barrie was wicket-keeping. 'If I strike the ball with even the slightest degree of impulse,' remarked the batsman, addressing the wicket-keeper, 'I shall immediately commence running with considerable velocity.' There was no occasion (adds Mr Barrie naively) for him to commence.
    W.G. GRACE
    Cricketing Reminiscences, 1899

Woolley whispered to the ball which at once hastened to the boundary just to please him.
    J.M. BARRIE

I saw 'Plum' Warner bat, I think, twice. On the first occasion he made one run, on the second he was not quite so successful.
    J.M. BARRIE

Barrie to Cardus at Lords:
You must come down to Stanway to watch me. I can bowl so slow that if I don't like a ball I can run after it and bring it back.
    NEVILLE CARDUS
    Autobiography, 1948

The Cricketer's Quotation Book

In after-tea matches at Stanway the keenest of all the players was Millie, the nursery-maid. No other fielder took such risks to keep runs down as this intrepid girl, who seldom used her hands but would intercept any ball with some portion or other of her anatomy.

Barrie: 'Why didn't you stop that ball with your hand Millie, instead of with your head?'
Millie: 'My head seemed to come more handy, Sir.'
   CYNTHIA ASQUITH
   Portrait of Barrie, 1954
   of J.M. Barrie

Hints to the team by their Captain:
Don't practise on opponents' ground before match begins. This can only give them confidence.

Should you hit the ball, run at once. Don't stop to cheer.

No batsman is allowed to choose his own bowler. You needn't think it.

If bowled first ball, pretend that you only came out for the fun of the thing, and then go away and sit by yourself behind the hedge.
   J.M. BARRIE
   Allahakbarries C.C., 1893

As for his own prowess – if that is the right word for it – one might tabulate it in some such manner as this. He knew everything about the theory of cricket, and could have chosen and directed the best team in the world. His slow, left-handed bowling – possibly the slowest that has yet been seen – was subtle, accurate, and maddeningly effective. His right-handed batting – for in games where both arms are employed he was always a right-hander – was almost uniformly unsuccessful. But perhaps his greatest distinction was the astounding courage with which he faced the fastest or most incalculable ball. For in those matches, as can well be imagined, it might appear from anywhere or at any velocity, and imperil any part of one's person. He never flinched. He hardly troubled to dodge. His calm was spectacular, and no violent or unexpected blow was ever seen to disturb it. It was the others who gasped, yelled, or shuddered, but never Barrie. Indomitable; there can be no other epithet to sum up the cricketing spirit in that small and fragile frame.

DENIS MACKAIL
The Story of J.M.B., 1941
on J.M. Barrie

Strolling about the theatre one evening he said on seeing me, 'Oh! Hicks, do you play cricket?'

I said, 'Yes I do, Mr Barrie.'

'Well, will you come down to Sandwich and play against the fire brigade men for me?' he inquired.

I said I should be delighted, but it would be impossible as I should be unable to get back to London in time to act at night.

'Oh, don't bother about that,' said Barrie, 'we can put on the understudy.'
> SUNDAY EXPRESS, 1939
> Sir Seymour Hicks recalling the time he played the part of Andrew McPhail, the medical student, in J.M. Barrie's play *Walker London* at Tooles' Theatre in 1892

My dear Wells
Certain Personal Matters of my own have got in the way of my thanking you for the copy of your book [*Certain Personal Matters*] which I do very heartily. I'm glad you collected those papers for many of them are long lost friends of mine, and furthermore the 'Veteran Cricketer' which is new strikes me of a heap. Not by its merit (pooh) but because I have you now; – You have a secret desire to spank them to leg and lift beauties to the off, and you probably can't, and so you are qualified for my cricket team. Elected whether you grumble or not.
> J.M. BARRIE
> letter to fellow author H.G. Wells, 1898

A guest at one dinner likened Barrie's after dinner speaking style, to 'Peter Pan at the speaker's wicket, making big hits off every ball'.
> E.V. LUCAS
> on J.M. Barrie

The Cricketer's Quotation Book

The Cricketer's Quotation Book

A BALLAD OF A PURELY IMAGINERY SHIP
Which may be called the 'Mary' because she brings the Cattle Home.

It was the Steamer 'Mary',
That sailed the wintry sea,
And the Captain had brought some big cigars
To keep him company.

Black was his hair as the raven's wing,
White were his clothes as snow,
And what went on in the Captain's mind
No-one will ever know.

For you couldn't call him a talkative man,
Even at Sunday prayers,
But – what means more to me and you –
He knew every inch of the bounding blue,
From Thames to Buenos Ayres.

And when he played at cricket,
He roused intense emotion
By hitting a sixer, now and then,
Into his favourite Ocean …

> VERSES BY E.V. LUCAS FROM A SOUVENIR OF A CRICKET MATCH BETWEEN PASSENGERS AND OFFICERS PLAYED ON BOARD THE BLUE STAR LINER *AVELONA*. AT SEA FEBRUARY 2ND, 1928

The sporadic character of first-class cricket has always been rather puzzling to me, and not less so since the invention of the motor-car has made it possible to see so much of England. There is good reason why Cumberland and Westmorland should not be too friendly to the game, because they are mountainous and attract rain. Rutland, of course, notoriously has not room for a cricket ground. Shropshire and Herefordshire are hilly. Devonshire gives way too much to a passion for moors. But why cannot eleven players of first-class quality be trained on the level meads of Wiltshire and Dorset, Berkshire and Oxfordshire, Hertfordshire and Huntingdonshire, Bedfordshire and Cambridgeshire, Suffolk and Norfolk? This is a great mystery. One does not want them necessarily to play all the other counties; one wants to know why cricket should be less ardently pursued in one county favourable to it than in another. One wants to know why the tide left a county. Did Norfolk's interest in cricket die with Fuller Pilch? Was it because there were no more Carpenters and Haywards that Cambridgeshire cooled?

E.V. LUCAS
Turning Things Over, 1929

There is no talk, none so witty and brilliant, that is so good as cricket talk, when memory sharpens memory, and the dead live again – the regretted, the forgotten – and the old happy days of burned out Junes revive.

ANDREW LANG

The Cricketer's Quotation Book

Amidst thy bowers the tyrant's hand is seen,
The rude pavilions sadden all they green;
One selfish pastime grasps the whole domain,
And half a faction swallows up the plain;
Adown thy glades, all sacrificed to cricket,
The hollow-sounding bat now guards the wicket;
Sunk are thy mounds in shapeless level all,
Lest aught impede the swiftly rolling ball;
And trembling, shrinking from the fatal blow,
Far, far away thy hapless children go.
The man of wealth and pride
Takes up a space that many poor supplied;
Space for the game, and all its instruments,
Space for pavilions and for scorers' tents;
The Ball, that raps his shins in padding cased,
Has wore the verdure to an arid waste;
His Park, where these exclusive sports are seen,
Indignant spurns the rustic from the green;
While through the plain, consigned to silence all,
In barren splendour flits the russet ball.
> LEWIS CARROLL
> 'The Deserted Parks'
> Notes by an Oxford Chiel, 1865–74

I delivered a simple ball which, I was told, had it gone far enough, would have been a wide.
> LEWIS CARROLL (CHARLES DODGSON)
> describing an occasion when he was asked to bowl

I see them in foul dug-outs, gnawed by rats,
And in the ruined temples, lashed by rain,
Dreaming of things they did with balls and bats.
   SIEGFRIED SASSOON
   'The Dreamers'

Oh, I am so glad you have begun to take an interest in cricket. It is simply a social necessity in England.
   P.G. WODEHOUSE
   Piccadilly Jim, 1918

Cricket is peculiarly a Christian game. No pagan nation has ever played it.
   MELBOURNE PAPER

Against Surrey, tomorrow, Somerset will beat Middlesex.
   LLOYD'S WEEKLY, 1909

It's a silly game that nobody wins.
   THOMAS FULLER

Watching cricket has given me more happiness than any other activity in which I have engaged. Lord's on a warm day, with a bottle, a mixed bag of sandwiches, and a couple of spare pipes in a despatch case, and I don't care who is playing whom. Cricket is the only game I can enjoy without taking sides.
   A.A. MILNE

The Cricketer's Quotation Book

Mʀ JACK HOBBS.

'Fender on Hobbs,' said a heading. It sounds like the opposite of the cricket on the hearth.
  PUNCH, 1925

A boy running hell for leather at Winchester cannoned head down into E.R. Wilson on his way to school, looked up, and in horror gasped 'Good God', to which E.R.W. gently replied, 'But strictly incognito'.
GEORGE LYTTELTON

Sir, the Eton and Harrow match is again at hand. May an imponderable quantity, who with countless other such, has suffered from four consecutive draws, venture a suggestion?

Whatever the rule, could it not be the practice in this match for the ingoing batsman always to leave the pavilion gate for the wicket as the outgoing batsman reaches the pavilion gate? Considering that there are 30 to 40 intervals on the fall of wickets, during each of which at least a minute (on the average) is lost, more than half an hour would be saved ...
JOHN GALSWORTHY
letter to *The Times*, 1926

ET IN ARCADIA

There was some grand cricket played in the period between the wars, and if our children and grandchildren condole with us in having lived in those dreadful times, we can at least answer, 'Ah, but we saw Chapman field, Larwood bowl, Hammond bat, and we are not so much to be pitied as you think.'
DUDLEY CAREW
To the Wicket, 1946

Jack Newman of Hampshire once appealed against the light and was turned down. Showing signs of dissent at the umpire's decision he was rebuked by his batting partner, his captain, the then Lionel Tennyson, who was at the other end of the pitch. Seeing that Newman was paying no attention, Tennyson shouted in annoyance: 'Can you hear me, Newman?' A reply was at last forthcoming. 'Yes, my Lord, but where are you speaking from?'
    DAVID RAYVERN ALLEN
    Cricket Extras, 1988

21 March, 1956 – Plum W. *will* fill his books with stuff like 'I shall never forget the wonderful hospitality of the Governor of N.S.W. and his gracious lady', which one could write without going nearer to N.S.W. than the lavatory at Victoria, when what would be of lasting Pepysian interest is to hear what Darling said to Trumper when he had a devilled cold pork-chop for breakfast on the morning of the Test Match – like that yokel Tom Wass when to his lbw appeal the umpire said 'not out' on the grounds that the ball would not have hit the stumps, Wass said 'It would a' had all three b——rs out of the ground'.
    GEORGE LYTTELTON
    The Lyttelton–Hart-Davis Letters, vol. 1, 1978.

AT LORD'S: JUNE 28, 3 p.m.

Sing a song of Woodfull,
Wiping England's eye;
Thirty-thousand people
'Neath a baking sky;
When 'Boy' Bradman opened
The ball began to sing;
Wasn't that a dainty dish
To set before the King?
  PUNCH, 1930

The Cricketer's Quotation Book

The bat is indescribable. A mass of willow, slightly rotten in places and resembling a mop at the bottom. The handle is said to be cane, but one player who has had a most extensive and varied acquaintance with canes, both at home and abroad, says that no cane *ever* stung like this bat, so it must be of some foreign substance. The balls go, some into the side windows of the school, some through those of the factory, others again attach themselves to the windows opposite.

    T.E. LAWRENCE
    on 'Playground Cricket'

Now this new kind of cricket takes courage to stick
    it,
There's bruises and fractures galore.
After kissing their wives and insuring their lives
Batsmen fearfully walk out to score.
With a prayer and curse, they prepare for the
    hearse,
Undertakers look on with broad grins.
Oh, they'd be a lot calmer in Ned Kelly's armour
When Larwood the wrecker begins.

    EXTRA VERSE TO SONG IN *OUR MISS GIBBS* AT HIS MAJESTY'S THEATRE, SYDNEY DURING 'BODYLINE' TOUR OF AUSTRALIA, 1932/33

The Cricketer's Quotation Book

First we went in, then they went in and we went in, and they went in, and they won. Then they went in and we went in, and they went in, and we went in, and we won. And then it were tea-time.

> H.B.T. WAKELAM
> recalling a village cricketer's reply, when asked, on his return from an 'away' match, how his team had fared, 1938

Can cricket be defined? You can see it, in perfect miniature, in the small, howling schoolboy, rushing from work some midsummer day, where an irritable master, who would fain perhaps himself be watching at Lord's, has been trying to supplant with Corn Laws or Equinoxes the crowded imagery of the cricket-stuffed mind – rushing from work to bat like Sutcliffe or bowl like Verity – noble imitation! Then to dream away the night in some fairy Test Match, where he has been chosen to bat first, and is just taking guard, when the morning bell clangs out the close of play!

> R.C. ROBERTSON-GLASGOW
> *Envoi*
> *The Brighter Side of Cricket*, 1933

Leave, O County Cricketer, leave for some fleeting moments, your perfect wicket, your 8 points, your struggle for first innings lead, your Bridge or Poker that goes on long after the rain has stopped, and the crowd has exhausted its patience and lost its shilling; come and watch us for nothing, and, if you have the heart to do it, come and laugh; if you have the soul, come and play.
    R.C. ROBERTSON-GLASGOW
    Village Cricket

I wish you'd speak to Mary, Nurse,
She's really getting worse and worse.
Just now when Tommy gave her out
She cried and then began to pout
And then she tried to take the ball
Although she cannot bowl at all.
And how she's standing on the pitch,
The miserable little Bitch!
    HILAIRE BELLOC
    'The Game of Cricket'

Those who write about cricket are often tempted into grandiose analogies but as a game it really is rather like the writing of a poem. What you do either works or does not and no one can tell you precisely wherein you have failed, nor can you know for certain if you will ever succeed, or, if you have succeeded, that you will ever do so again. The failure is in you, it is you that is getting in your own way.
    P.J. KAVANAGH
    The Mystery of Cricket, 1981

The last bowler to be knighted was Sir Francis Drake.
  ARTHUR MAILEY
  Reminiscences

Most would agree that Parliament must continue to exist. While it does so, the two parties must play a game modelled, apparently, on that of cricket; a game in which no innings can be prolonged for ever.
  C. NORTHCOTE PARKINSON
  The Law of Delay

Mr Richard Wainwright my M.P. is concerned about the omission of Mr D'Oliveira from the M.C.C. South African party.

I have asked him to take up with the Race Relations Board about the omission of Messrs. Binks, Hutton and Sharpe, which appears to be a clear case of discrimination against the Yorkshire race.
  MR W. GETHING
  letter to *The Times*, 2nd Sept. 1968

Mr Nicholas Scott is one of the leading batsmen for Lord's and Commons cricket. It is therefore unthinkable that he should be dislodged by his constituency ... Cricket is more important than the niceties of Tory politics.
  AYTON WHITAKER, 1977
  The Way to Lord's, Cricketing Letters to *The Times*, 1983

Who is this man, with creaking bones,
This ancient, uttering oaths and groans,
Bowling round-arms, and that most vilely?
Sir, 'tis the ghost of Bill O'Reilly.
   SIR ROBERT MENZIES

Australian P.M. Mr Curtin came to Lord's in 1944. In a speech he said: 'Australians will always fight for these twenty-two yards. Lord's and its traditions belong to Australia just as much as to England'.
   SIR PELHAM WARNER
   Lord's

Cricket? It civilizes people and creates good gentlemen. I want everyone to play cricket in Zimbabwe. I want ours to be a nation of gentlemen.
>ROBERT MUGABE
>Prime Minister of Zimbabwe

Cricket can be a bridge and a glue ...
Cricket for peace is my mission.
>PRESIDENT ZIA OF PAKISTAN

'Mrs Thatcher is in the position of a Martian trying to understand cricket,' said Neil Kinnock referring to her attitude towards Football identity cards and the Taylor enquiry.
>JOHN CARVER
>*The Guardian*, 21 April 1989

A catch was hit very hard to point, which Mr Adams secured (though it nearly knocked him over), but the batsman not wishing to leave the wicket, where he had greatly enjoyed himself, appealed to the umpire at that end, who happened to be Mr Justice Manisty. That learned judge at once called the eleven in the field and the umpire at the other end, making twelve in all, together and addressed them thus: 'Gentlemen, I have the highest, possible opinion of your impartiality, your patriotism, your knowledge of the game, your unflinching resolution never to call a ball which is not a bump ball a bump ball, or any other opprobrious name, but to do your duty without fear or favour. I ask you, in full reliance of your noble qualities, and with a most confident belief in your infallibility, was this a catch or not?' To this stirring appeal the twelve replied as one man, 'It was'. 'Then', said Mr Justice Manisty, 'all I've got to say is, it's not out!'

> J.W. GOLDMAN
> *Cricketers and the Law*, 1958

Surely Mr Adlard achieves a masterpiece of meiosis in saying that Gilbert Jessop 'should be included among the mighty hitters'? It is like saying that St. Peter's must find a place among the big churches of the world.

> LAURENCE MEYNELL, 1953

Charles Wright was Captain of Notts, and had also got a century in the University match. He was a most delightful person, but by no means the complete *Encyclopaedia Britannica*.

> CYRIL FOLEY
> *The Cricketer*, 1927

Easy to watch, difficult to bowl to, and impossible to write about. When you bowled to him there weren't enough fielders; when you wrote about him there weren't enough words.

> R.C. ROBERTSON-GLASGOW
> *Cricket Prints*, 1943
> writing about Frank Woolley

Cricket is a batsman's game. The City of London has never emptied to watch a bowler as it did to watch Bradman.
   E.W. SWANTON

They vanish, these immortal players, and we suddenly realize with astonishment that years have passed since we heard a passing mention of some of them. At one point they seem as much a part of the permanent scheme of things as the sun which glows upon their familiar faces and attitudes and the grass which makes the background for their portrait; and then, bless us, it is time even for them to go.
   EDMUND BLUNDEN
   Cricket Country, 1944

Caldicott: That German Officer looked a lot like old Dickie Randall. You know him, used to bowl slow leg-breaks. He played for the Gentlemen once – caught and bowled for duck as I remember.

Charters: You think he's a traitor then?

Caldicott: But he played for the Gentlemen!

Charters: Ah, but only once.

   Night Train to Munich, 1940 [film]
   written by Frank Launder & Sidney Gilliat
   directed by Carol Reed

Cricket is a game full of forlorn hopes and sudden dramatic changes of fortunes, and its rules are so ill-defined that their interpretation is partly an ethical business. It is not a 20th century game and nearly all modern-minded people dislike it.
>GEORGE ORWELL
>'Raffles and Miss Blandish', 1944

St. Cyprian's School Magazine: 1914 Season. Characters of the 1st XI: BLAIR – has improved very much of late ... should with care bat very well. He catches well, but must learn to move more quickly. Can bowl a little.
>MICHAEL SHELDEN
>*Orwell: The Authorized Biography*

Though wayward Time be changeful as Man's Will
We have the game, we have the Oval still,
And still the Gas-Works mark the Gas-Works End
And still the sun shines and the rain descends
>JOHN MASEFIELD
>'Eighty-Five to Win'

Tha' knows one thing I learned about cricket: tha' can't put in what God left out. Tha' sees two kinds of cricketers, them that uses a bat as if they are shovelling muck and them that plays proper and like as not God showed both of 'em how to play.
>WILFRED RHODES
>quoted in *Cricket Mad* (1959) by Michael Parkinson

The Cricketer's Quotation Book

It wasn't cricket; it wasn't cricket that an elderly gnome-like individual with a stringy neck and creaking joints should, by dint of head-work and superior cunning, reverse the proverb that youth will be served. It was an ascendancy of brain over brawn, of which, like a true Englishman, I felt suspicious.
    L.P. HARTLEY
    The Go-Between, 1953

The Cricketer's Quotation Book

A professional cricketer told his captain, just before a match, that he could not play owing to a busted finger. Neville Cardus was called in as consultant and, after examining the slightly discoloured forefinger-nail, said, 'Joe, you're supposed to be a slow spin bowler – not Kreisler'.
    SPORTS EDITOR
    London Evening News, 1950

To go to a cricket match for nothing but cricket is as though a man were to go into an inn for nothing but drink.
    NEVILLE CARDUS
    Cricket all my Days

Midsummer Day 1956   *Lord's Pavilion*

(1) Cardus. A *delightful* present indeed. At his best – and he often is – there is no writer on any game to touch him. And I join issue with you – and him – as to his early work being inferior. You have cleverly left out his over-ripe period – the tour in Australia of '46–'47.

(2) This is just to cheer you with the news that I see no chance of writing a letter till Sunday. Here all day watching, and rest of day talking. I am at the moment surrounded with Forsytes – whiskered, jowly, Tory, querulous, magnificently fatuous and fundamentally imperishable, thank God.

(3) Later from ground. I have been asked to play. May has leprosy, Cowdrey swallowed a bit of egg-shell at breakfast and the surgeon will be here

The Cricketer's Quotation Book

shortly, Richardson has been stung by a bumble-bee but will almost certainly be fit for the Oval match, Evans cut himself shaving, Graveney's mother has lumbago. So have I, but there is literally no-one else.

(4) At 9.55 there was a queue outside the ground from Swiss Cottage, any number under thirty years of age.

(5) Roman society was ruined by *'panem et circenses'*, i.e. Test Matches, Football pools, and high wages. *Verb sap.*

>GEORGE LYTTELTON
>*The Lyttelton Hart-Davis Letters, Vol. 1*,
>1978

The Cricketer's Quotation Book

I passed him [Cowdrey] and Bailey as they went in on Friday morning. I murmured 'Good luck'. Cowdrey said 'Thank you, sir'; Bailey said nothing. In five balls Bailey was out and in five hours Cowdrey had made 152. The god of cricket likes good manners.
    GEORGE LYTTELTON
    June 1957
    The Lyttelton Hart-Davis Letters, Vol. 2, 1979

Clearly the gods rule cricket, and to that extent I am in tune with the deepest influences on the game. A spot of rain, a flash of sun, a swathe of wind, a flick of hail, a yield of earth, a tuft of turf, an errant mole, a humid noon, a pollen surge – all or any of these natural and uncontrollable forces of the weather can be crucial. Cricket is the rawest game left on the planet.
    MELVYN BRAGG
    On the Boundary, 1981

If as I fear, there is cricket in heaven, there will also, please God, be rain.
    ARTHUR MARSHALL

The Colonel, like so many myopic cricketers, failed to observe that seagulls face the wind!
    MALCOLM ELWIN

Some people use sheep: I bowl. Along the years, lying in my bed, I must have sent down hundreds of overs – leg-breaks, mostly, mixed with my own version of the googly. If I am rarely successful, either at taking wickets or at inducing sleep, this does not make me feel wretched. I enjoy the rhythm, persistent, floating ... and since everything can be contained in the reading of a wicket, my thoughts are seldom pierced by dark knives in the night.

MICHAEL HOLROYD
Not Cricket (Summer Days), 1981

The telephones had rung in chorus. The duty controller from Jodrell conveyed a businesslike message that the Russians had 'launched a rocket which would reach the moon on Sunday evening'. The voice on the house phone was that of an excited pressman asking what we were 'going to do about it'. My answer was brief: 'I am going to play cricket'.

BERNARD LOVELL
The Moon Match, 1981

When Lancashire and Gloucestershire invented pyjama cricket in a 1971 cup match at Old Trafford, there was a suggestion to the umpire that it might be too dark to carry on. 'You can see the moon.' Arthur Jepson replied, 'How far do you want to see?'

A 'War of the Roses' cricket match was played (at Stratford) in which Peggy Ashcroft led the Lancastrians and I the Yorkists. Her team had Cyril Washbrook as honorary captain and mine had Len Hutton. You need to know your history to appreciate why Brewster Mason as the Earl of Warwick was the Umpire. Politically the result of the match had to be a draw.
> DONALD SINDEN
> *Laughter in the Second Act*

If we had all our friends checked at cricket matches we'd have no friends and no cricket.
> JOHN LE CARRÉ
> *A Perfect Spy*

The atmosphere reminded me of a minor public school ... On the face of it, life was a mixture of the quaint and the archaic. Every year the Office virtually closed to attend the Lord's Test Match where MI5 had an unofficial patch in the Lord's Tavern.
> PETER WRIGHT
> *Spycatcher*, 1987

Sometimes I dream of revolution, a bloody coup d'état by the second rank – troupes of actors slaughtered by their understudies, magicians sawn in half by indefatigably smiling glamour girls, cricket teams wiped out by marauding bands of twelfth men.
> MOON in Tom Stoppard's *The Real Inspector Hound*, 1968

They've started this filthy floodlit cricket with cricketers wearing tin hats and advertisements for contraceptives on their boots.
>   TOBY
>   in Alan Ayckbourn's *A Gardener in Love*,
>   *Intimate Exchanges*, 1985

When we were living in Sydney a friend told me that one night, while she and her husband were making love, she suddenly noticed something sticking in his ear. When she asked him what it was he replied, 'Be quiet! I'm listening to the cricket.'
>   VICKY RANTZEN
>   *The Observer*, 1978

I don't know if I prefer Rog to have a good innings or a bad one: if it's a good one, he relives it in bed, shot by shot, and if it's a bad one he actually replays the shots until he gets it right. He can make a really good innings last all winter.
>   MIRIAM
>   in Richard Harris's *Outside Edge*, 1980

Cricket teams ... share a face that belongs to a prefect's father, who has entertained loads of clients.
>   ROBERT ROBINSON
>   *Prescriptions of a Pox Doctor's Clerk*, 1970–90

The Cricketer's Quotation Book

BIRTH CONTROL

Of recent years women have been taking to cricket more and more, and the following suggestions, which I flatter myself are eminently practical, while being also romantic, show how the problem of England's cricketing future should be tackled.

The MCC (stand up, please, as a mark of respect) should appoint a select committee to draw up a list of all the best men and women cricketers and should endeavour to arrange suitable alliances between them. This is putting it very much in a nutshell, as I quite realize that it will be a tricky business and require much knowledge and tact. It may be wrong, for instance, to assume that the union of a male fast and a female googly bowler will produce an unplayable type embodying the pace of one and the finger spin of the other. Breeders of high-class bloodstock will tell you that the mating of two extremes, a stayer and a sprinter, seldom achieves the happy medium, which, theoretically, it should do. It will, therefore, be necessary to co-opt. I think, one or two members of the Jockey Club on the Committee.

Of course, this is all going to cost money, and I would suggest that the MCC (pause for silent prayer) set aside a special fund for the purpose. Those who, with the committee's approval, propose getting married would receive a small grant on signing bills of lading or whatever the term is, and a substantial sum on each male child produced. It is obvious that most money must be given on the COD basis, because you can't trust some of these young men nowadays. Very briefly, such is my proposal for the betterment of English cricket. It will take time and labour, but the results will surely justify themselves.

I forgot to add that the fees of the members of the committee should be about £500 per year each. I am prepared to serve on it.

>   J.C. CLAY
>   quoted in *Cricket: Pleasures of Life*, 1953 by John Arlott

I well remember ... at my Big School, after I missed a catch at long-leg, saying to myself 'O Lord take away my life, for I am not worthy to live!'

>   JOHN COWPER POWYS
>   *Autobiography*

For my own sake too I wished that time might stop; that I might stand for ever in the sun, while the trees rustled and the young voices laughed along the terrace, and watch my darling so beautiful and happy at his play. But time slipped on, and my darling started to sweat like a cart-horse, and the Scholars were faced with shameful defeat.
SIMON RAVEN
Fielding Gray, 1969

The English, not being a religious people, invented cricket to give them an idea of eternity.
ANDRÉ MAUROIS

Cricket, like the upper classes and standards in general, is in permanent decline. No-one would have it otherwise.
ALAN ROSS

Distrusting the arts, the English found a substitute in cricket – a timeless blend of formal dancing, rhetoric and comic opera. If we allow, as Cardus contended, that cricket is an art form, then it must be permitted its high priest, one who will truly comprehend its mysteries, regard it with an indulgent affection and seek to perpetuate its golden hours.
KENNETH GREGORY
Cricket's Last Romantic

Cricket is an art, a means of national expression. Voltaire says that no one is so boring as the man who insists on saying everything ... But I believe I owe it to the many who did not see the Edgbaston innings to say that I thought it showed of the directions that, once freed, the West Indies might take. The West Indies, in my view, embody more sharply than elsewhere Nietzche's conflict between the ebullience of Dionysius and the discipline of Apollo. Kanhai's going crazy might seem to be Dionysius in us breaking loose. It was absent from Edgbaston. Instead, the phrases which go nearest to expressing what I saw and have reflected upon are those of Lytton Strachey on French Literature: '[the] mingled distinction, gaiety and grace which is one of the unique products of the mature poetical genius of France'.

    C.L.R. JAMES
    KANHAI: A STUDY IN CONFIDENCE, 1966

Writing critically about West Indies cricket and cricketers, or any cricket for that matter, is a difficult discipline. The investigation, the analysis, even the casual historical or sociological gossip about any great cricketer should deal with his actual cricket, the way he bats or bowls or fields, does all or any of these. You may wander far from where you have started, but unless you have your eyes constantly on the ball, in fact, never take your eyes off it, you are soon writing not about cricket, but yourself (or other people) and psychological or literary responses to the game. This can be done and has been done quite brilliantly, adding a little something to literature but practically nothing to cricket, as little as the story of Jack and the Beanstalk (a great tale) adds to our knowledge of agriculture. This is particularly relevant to the West Indies.

>C.L.R. JAMES
>*Kanhai: A Study in Confidence* (New World, Guyana, 1966)

West Indies cricket has spent a long time shaking off the unflattering stereotypes perpetuated by tabloid headlines such as: 'Calypso collapso' and 'Carnival cricketers'.

It was a reputation even accepted for a time by West Indians themselves, summed up in verse by one of the Caribbean's popular poets, Edward Kamau Brathwaite: 'But I say it once and I say it again, when things going good you can't hold we but let murder start and, old man, you can't find a man to hold up de side'.

>TONY COZIER
>*The Independent*, March 1994

Worrell has immense natural dignity. No cricketer since Hammond has had such sheer presence as he takes the field. The petty things of cricketing life seem to be below Worrell. The will to win at all costs is somehow distasteful to him. The game, not the result, means more.

>RON ROBERTS

Denis Compton had a specially warm memory of an aged coloured gentleman of the old school, who having enjoyed the three 'Ws' to the full, plucked slyly at his elbow as he stood in the deep.

'Mistah Compton,' said this ancient, 'Mistah Worrell, Mistah Weekes and Mistah Walcott comes first, den comes de Lord above.'
IAN PEEBLES

Benaud says that Griffith throws (he has to fill his column somehow), but E.W. Swanton is indignant about this (properly so) and concludes by saying, he will return to the subject 'in a calmer moment'. Now, there is a *real* pro – he gets *two* columns out of it. And, of course, the whole ... is very, very soothing to *Telegraph* readers.
Punch, 1965

A Lament for Hope and Glory
We knew they were doomed from the moment they moved into a commanding position. It was as if the Light Brigade, having survived everything the enemy could hurl against them during their hapless charge on the Russian guns, had looked up to see a Soviet main battle tank bearing down on them, its turret rotating ominously in their direction.

Perhaps a better image would be that of the neutron bomb. Curtly Ambrose, the nuclear-tipped West Indies strike bowler, did not so much destroy England during last week's third Test match in Trinidad, he virtually removed all trace of them from the game ...

The Cricketer's Quotation Book

By close of play on Tuesday, having been set a target to win of just 194, England were 40 for eight off 14.5 overs. It was a collapse even more humiliating than that of John Major over voting rights in Brussels.

Next morning, England's remaining wickets were taken quicker than a stray fiver in the Portobello Road. There were by now enough ducks on the field to feed an average family for a fortnight ...

Lord have mercy. English cricket, once a byword for order and efficiency, with sporadic exhibitions of genius, is today – as Sir Denis Thatcher might crisply put it – about as much use as a one-legged man at an arse-kicking party.

>Profile of the England Cricket Team
>*The Sunday Times*, April 1994

A second boundary, taken off the hip by a shaky batsman [Hick], had roughly the effect on Ambrose that the sight of alcohol seems to have on ayatollahs.

>PETER ROEBUCK
>*The Sunday Times*, April, 1994

Here was English cricket's Messiah, preceded by Ian Botham's shaggy John the Baptist. Perhaps we should all have noticed that Hick became eligible to play for England on April Fool's day. Five months later, the self-assured 25-year-old batsman had turned into a Wilfred Owen-style shambling soldier, traumatised by heavy artillery.

>JOHN DUGDALE ON GRAEME HICK
>Feuds Corner, *The Sunday Times*, 3 April 1994

The Cricketer's Quotation Book

Watching Graeme Hick yesterday – not at his most iridescent but still over-qualified for the game everyone else was playing – recalled the story about an attendant at Florence's Uffizi Gallery. 'Remember, Signor,' he told an American tourist, 'here it is not the paintings that are on trial.'

MICHAEL HENDERSON
The Guardian, 21 July 1988
Worcs. v. Yorks. at Worcester

At his fastest, off the long run, he moved up in a curve, swerving slightly out, round the umpire. His coaches had adjusted a few details of his action but fundamentally it was as natural as it was splendid. He stalked back to his mark, arms bowed, at a threateningly muscle-bound gait: but as soon as he gathered himself and began his run he became a different creature. About this time someone described him as a young bull; and there was in his approach that majestic rhythm that emerges as a surprise in the Spanish fighting bull. It steps out of the toril, stands hesitant, cumbersome then, suddenly, sights the peon from the cuadrilla, pulls itself up and sets off towards him in a mounting glory of rhythm, power and majesty. Such was the run up of the young Trueman as, body thrown forward, he moved first at a steady pad and gradually accelerated, hair flopping, and swept into the delivery process. Again the analogy of the bull holds good, for the peak of its charge is controlled violence, precisely applied in a movement of rippling speed. Trueman's body swung round so completely that the batsman saw his left shoulder blade: the broad left foot was, for an infinitesimal period of time, poised to hammer the ground. He was a cocked trigger, left arm pointed high, head steady, eyes glaring at the batsman as that great stride widened, the arm slashed down and as the ball was fired down the pitch, his body was thrown hungrily after it, the right toe raking the ground closely beside the wicket as he swept on. Coming in almost from behind, the umpire threw his left shoulder up and helped him to deliver from so near the stumps that sometimes he brushed the umpire. Indeed once, when Sam Pothecary was standing at Taunton, Trueman felled him, as he passed, with a blow of his steel right toe-cap on the ankle so savage as to leave that mildest of umpires limping for a fortnight.

JOHN ARLOTT
Fred, 1971

Fred Trueman tells a story of a Yorkshire cricketer who began to get ideas above his station after being awarded his England cap. The trip to Lord's changed him completely and he returned to play for his county entertaining thoughts of marrying the daughter of the President of MCC. On the morning of his first match with the county after playing for England, he looked out of his bedroom window and said: 'The rain is terrestrial'. His team mate looked dumbfounded.

'Surely, tha' means torrential' he said. The new England player shrugged his shoulders. 'It's all imperial to me,' he said.
>MICHAEL PARKINSON
>'Snobbery in Sport', *Punch*, 1969

His public were the customers whose quiet contemplation of their evening pint was suddenly converted, in an instant, into participation in the Greatest Show on (Cricket's) Earth. The one and only F.S. Trueman had arrived. Fred's jacket was suddenly thrust to the back of his shoulders, the chin jutted, the pipe projected even further as he hustled to the bar. Henry Irving never made a greater impact with a stage entrance than Freddie Trueman in a pub.
>JOHN HAMPSHIRE
>*Family Argument*, 1983

The modern cricketer is not an ogre, nor is he deliberately obstructive. Although in most cases it would be unfair to dismiss him as a spoiled brat, he is too often lazy, ill-disciplined and reluctant to put in the effort and dedication commensurate with the wages he is earning. He has a very low boredom threshold with a constant need to be told what to do with his time.
>BOB WILLIS
>*Lasting the Pace*, 1985

We are nostalgic for the game's past, as well as our own. Some day, I suppose, some will look fondly back on boozy, can-rattling spectators, players' rude and self-congratulatory gestures, shirts proper to squash net cricket, helmets less appropriate to Lord's than to Squires Gate.
ROY FULLER
From Sparrow Park to Stanley Park, 1981

Alas, I don't even know enough about cricket to attack it. Anyway, I wouldn't attack it as I much prefer it to the muddied oafs.
GRAHAM GREENE

The gum-chewing habit is very catching, and you will sometimes see a whole fielding team resembling a herd of cows at pasture.
R.C. ROBERTSON-GLASGOW
Crusoe on Cricket, 1966

I would rather watch a man at his toilet than on a cricket field, but such is the madness of the players that in time they come to believe that the spectacle they make of themselves dressed in white wielding a willow (to use their own revolting phraseology – and why not?) is something their betters should pay to see.
ROBERT MORLEY
Death to the Flannelled Fools

The Cricketer's Quotation Book

As a substitute for music, I watch ballet; the dance, for me, is music made visible. Cricket I watch for almost the same reason, except that its music, so to speak, is abstract ... I see the game as ceremony.
DAVID WRIGHT
A Deaf Man Looks at Cricket, 1981

Ah, cricket, the sight of bowler and players genuinely applauding a century against them. If a Rangers soccer side stood to applaud a Celtic goal I'd know the age of miracles had come. Cricket's greatness lies in the ability of players to honour a foe. It's the way life should be lived.
PROFESSOR WILLIAM BARCLAY

But after all, it's not the winning that matters, is it? Or is it? It's – to coin a word – the amenities that count: the smell of the dandelions, the puff of the pipe, the click of the bat, the rain on the neck, the chill down the spine, the slow, exquisite coming on of sunset and dinner and rheumatism.
ALASTAIR COOKE

Cricket needs umpires who grace the general scene with sartorial sharpness, instead of resembling a pair of Balkan refugees clad by Oxfam.
JOHN SHEPPARD
The Cricketer, 1974

The Cricketer's Quotation Book

Can't stand those fellas who jump on a bowler when he's taken a wicket. It's like assistants at Harrods mobbing a chap when he's sold a tie.
HENRY COTTON

The Revd David Sheppard (now Bishop of Liverpool) had managed to get very little practice before the England tour to Australia in 1962–63. He dropped a number of chances at slip. Fred Trueman, never short of advice, could not restrain his feelings when yet another snick went to ground: 'You might keep yer eyes shut when yer prayin', Vicar, but I wish you'd keep 'em open when I'm bowling!'
FRED TRUEMAN TO DAVID SHEPPARD

Bill Hudson lost 100 schooners of beer when he bet that Kevin Douglas Walters could not make 100 first time out against the Poms. Only when you have seen him bat and tested his self-possession do you realise how rash that wager really was.
IAN WOOLDRIDGE
The Cricketer, 1966

It seems that neutral umpires were not used until about 1836 and, hitherto, provided the umpire was a gentleman of good repute, no objection would be taken to his having placed a bet on his team. It would be a point of honour with him to carry out his duties impartially. In this respect times have changed; eyebrows would certainly be raised now, even though Messrs Bird and Constant are gentlemen of good

repute, if it became known that they had each placed £1,000 with Ladbrokes on England to win the first Test next summer against Pakistan in which they were both to officiate!
GORDON ROSS
The Cricketer, 1978

Cricket must be the only business where you can make more money on one day than three.
PAT GIBSON
Daily Express, 1975

Sir, Today I learned with interest that the average height of our current Test side is 6 feet. Since there are 11 playing members of the team their total length is therefore 66 feet or 22 yards – the length of the wicket. Is this significant?
MRS PATRICIA CROZIER
letter to *The Times*, Sept. 1978

I used to enjoy cricket, except for one game during the holidays when we were playing up against a telegraph pole. I was the stumper and when I turned suddenly to stop a ball, I hit that pole and broke one of my front teeth clean in two. It was with me for ages because there wasn't any question of going to the dentist. You had to pay for the dentist and we didn't have any money.
JOE GORMLEY
former NUM President in *Battered Cherub*

The Cricketer's Quotation Book

Sir, I was horrified to learn the other day that there is now a cricket club in Finland. I left England twenty-five years ago to get away from people like yourself. Is nowhere sacred?
>DOCTOR K, ENGLISH DEPARTMENT, HELSINKI UNIVERSITY
>letter to editor of *The Helsinki Cricketer*

Hello, Dolly,
This is Lord's, Dolly,
Just to tell you that it's not because you're brown.
Oh dear me no, Dolly,
You could go, Dolly,
But you can't bat in the sunshine, and you might let us down.

But please turn white, Dolly,
Overnight, Dolly,
And we'll hold another meeting in the Pav.,
Then we'll find, Dolly,
We've had a change of mind, Dolly,
But not until you change the skin you have.
>TERRY DELANEY
>adaptation of title song from the musical *Hello Dolly*, 1968

The Cricketer's Quotation Book

First match – opened the bowling – rock concert – blaring away in next field – amorous labradors – making love at leg-slip – street arabs – playing footie at deep fine leg – play stopped – not rain – fire – fire engines on pitch – crowd of several hundred – new flannels all black smuts – no-balled few times in first over – should have gone round the wicket – should have have gone Lord's – Lancashire in Gillette final – had the tickets – gave them away when captain asked me to open – had a bath, and drank fourteen pints – best bitter – great game, cricket.

STANLEY REYNOLDS
'Opening for Dreamshire or A Yank on the Greensward', *Punch*, 1973

In the cricket season, I learned that there was a safe and far-away place on the field called 'deep' which I always chose. When 'over' was called, I simply went more and more 'deep' until I was sitting on the steps of the pavilion reading the plays of Nöel Coward, whom I had got on to after Bulldog Drummond.

JOHN MORTIMER

I have often thought how much better a life I would have had, what a better man I would have been, how much healthier an existence I would have led, if I had been a cricketer instead of an actor.

LORD OLIVIER

Len Hutton was going to show me around Manchester, but he didn't know how to charter a boat – it's been raining up there.
>   FRANK SINATRA
>   *Show Band Show*

When I was watching Fred Astaire I used to think, here was a chap who would have been a great batsman.
>   SIR LEONARD HUTTON

The grass has a Mohican cut
playing cricket for the Sunday Sinners
I steal a single with a baseball bunt –

in the pavilion
Denis shunts forward in my vacant seat
and on the flip side of my pencilled poem
like swansdown on a stagnant pond
doodles in beautiful italic script:

musicians on a cathedral crawl
Coventry Canterbury and Rome
anacreontic madrigals and Keats' nightingales
blowing out one last organ stop of sadness –
they look down on the marbled marquetry
and hear the strangest cry 'The Hyriads' –

I leg it back to the pavilion
marvel at the calligraphy
erase my HB poem
Denis defecting to the Saints
had vanished in a whiff of aftershave
leaving me his inspiration like a donor card.
>   MICHAEL HENRY
>   'Stagnant Pond'

It's a funny kind of month, October. For the really keen cricket fan, it's when you realise that your wife left you in May.
>   DENIS NORDEN

Is there no way in which Richards of Hampshire could be co-opted into the English Test side? Can no patriotic English girl be persuaded to marry him? He is quite personable and surely such a sacrifice would qualify him for selection. Failing that, could not some elderly gentleman adopt him?
>   NED SHERRIN
>   producer, director, writer and performer
>   letter to *The Times*

In 1982, Dr Israr Ahmed, a Pakistani theologian, was one of the instigators in a move by the military government to forbid men from watching women's sporting events in case unseemly passions were aroused. He aired the view that cricket was 'a game of eunuchs which wastes the nation's precious time'.

The Cricketer's Quotation Book

Difficult to be more laid back without being actually comatose.
>   FRANCES EDMONDS ON DAVID GOWER
>   *Daily Express*, 1985

It was, perhaps, inevitable that your God-given talent should be envied by those who sweat in shell-suits to achieve less dazzling results. But who would have believed that spite and stupidity could have so hijacked the glorious game? Corinth, it seems, has given way to Chelmsford and we are all the poorer for it.
>   FRANCES EDMONDS ON DAVID GOWER
>   *The Independent*, 1994

[Gower wore] an expression of permanent pained bewilderment, 'like a man who's just stepped into a lift-shaft.'

The riposte followed – a sumptuous square-cut which unfolded like a royal carpet all the way to the boundary.
>   MICHAEL HENDERSON
>   *The Guardian*, 23 April 1988
>   On Gower in Derby. v. Leics.

The game you are frightened of losing is not worth winning.
>   BENNY GREEN

During the I.C.C. Trophy many of the teams conversed on the field in foreign tongues with the odd cricket phrase coming through in English. One such side was Israel – a really happy band of village standard players – from whose chatter I suddenly picked up the term 'in-swinger'. On asking their Jewish captain as to why he had no translation for this type of delivery, he informed me that this was because nobody bowled it in the Old Testament.
GORDON HEWITT
'The Good, The Bad and The Ridiculous' *The Cricketer*, 1994

It was not unlike watching Lazarus rise from the dead and get mown down by a runaway truck on his way to meet his mates in the bar.
IAN WOOLDRIDGE
Daily Mail
on New Zealand's performance v. Pakistan, World Cup, 1992

The advent of a mosque with its burnished copper dome has made navigation towards (Lord's) much easier for people coming from that direction (Regent's Park). There was a brief period when the muezzin's amplified calls to prayer could be heard tantalisingly in the middle of the cricket pitch, but that all stopped after local inhabitants had secured an injunction against the romantic but distinctly alien sound.
GEOFFREY MOORHOUSE
Lord's, 1983

The Cricketer's Quotation Book

[Courtney Walsh], who has effectively lost West Indies both their matches, was presented with a carpet for not running out Salim Jaffer off the final ball. He was last seen trying to fly home on it.
MARTIN JOHNSON
The Independent, 1987

He looks like and bats like a librarian: a prodder a nudger, with a virile bottom hand that works the ball to the on side, and a top hand for keeping his other glove on.
MIKE SELVEY
The Guardian, 4 March 1988
on Bert Vance's Test debut, 3rd Test New Zealand v. England at Wellington

Robin Williams the elastic-faced American comic actor, got the royal grin when he opined to Prince Charles after a recent charity concert: 'Cricket is basically baseball on valium'.
THE SUNDAY TIMES, 20 MARCH 1988

On the lack of Test Match coverage from Australia: 'It's enough to make an Orthodox Jew want to join the Nazi Party.'
JUDGE MICHAEL ARGYLE
at the Old Bailey

The Cricketer's Quotation Book

It is paradoxical the way the opposition to the government is coming from the most unexpected quarters. But then I like that sort of thing. I'm the sort of person who likes to play cricket in Northern Greenland.
> LORD SHACKLETON ON THE LORDS
> *The Guardian*, 30 April 1988

Alan Green, the occasional off-spinner, might just turn a spin-drier but not much else.
> MIHIR BOSE
> *The Sunday Times*, 12 June 1988

Cricket on pitches like this bears the same relationship to true first-class cricket that target shooting bears to Russian roulette.
> MALCOLM WINTER
> *Sunday Times*, 12 June 1988
> Northants v. West Indies, Northampton

Barring injuries or sexual indiscretions between now and next Thursday, the three other newcomers [*Barnett, Russell and Lawrence*] seem certain to get the benefit of the Peter May Emporium's Giant 1988 England Cap Sale.
> MATTHEW ENGEL
> *The Guardian*, 20 Aug. 1988

Watching Clinton steal a match in which Hick and Botham are playing is like going to a Pavarotti concert and seeing him upstaged by Des O'Connor. He is inelegant: a shoveller, scooper, nudger and smearer for whom the V between mid-off and mid-on is an exclusion zone. But he knows how to pace an innings and keep things ticking.
>MIKE SELVEY
>Surrey v. Worcs., Oval, B & H Cup
>*The Guardian*, 3 May 1989

If it is embarrassing then it is wrong, but if it is private, and hopefully delightful, then what could be better – even in the middle of a Test Match?
>TED DEXTER
>on players' nocturnal activities in wake of the Gatting 'barmaid' incident, 1989

Any cricketer would want to bowl to Bradman even if he were to hit them for six. It's the same with Robin.
>BRIAN WALDEN
>writer and former MP on Robin Day and the politicians queuing to be lashed by his tongue
>John Diamond *The Sunday Times*, 4 June 1989

Professional coaching is a man trying to get your legs close together when other men had spent a lifetime trying to get them wider apart.
>RACHAEL HEYHOE FLINT
>displaying her customary flair for sound bites

The Cricketer's Quotation Book

'Ee man, there's been a lot of stotty cap today,' a spectator remarked on the boundary at Durham.

This, it emerged, was a reference to the number of apparent catches which were actually off a bump-ball. Don't think I will ever come to terms with this north-east lingo.
> SIMON HUGHES
> 'Cricketer's Diary', *The Independent*, 4 Aug. 1993

So I joined a Barclays Bank graduate training scheme in 1991. People were amazed I could contemplate such a swap. I suppose it was like John Major running away from his circus background to be an accountant.
> JOHN CARR
> on his leaving of Middlesex
> As reported by Rob Steen, *The Independent*, Aug. 1993

Explaining the rules of cricket is an excellent test for high-powered brains.
> PRIME MINISTER JOHN MAJOR
> to a symposium of the world's major bankers
> *The Independent*, 1994

The players have said it is not much fun when you can taste the fog.
> TED DEXTER
> Calcutta, 1992–3 Indian tour

The Cricketer's Quotation Book

[Ted Dexter] the most charismatic cricketer of his generation, who used to roar thro' the Lord's gates on a 1,000cc motor-bike, will phut-phut his way back out of them on a metaphorical moped, his public persona having altered – in the space of four and a half years – from a latter day Lawrence of Arabia into something closer to Mr Magoo.
    MARTIN JOHNSON
    The Independent, Aug. 1993

Four separate stoppages for rain and bad light left the day as shapeless as a Demis Roussos costume.
    GLENN MOORE
    The Independent, 1994
    Kent v. Middx., Canterbury

The Cricketer's Quotation Book

His cricket is a disgraceful collection of outrages, unfit for normal society and yet effective in the deciding of matches. Few players can have made so much of so little; precious few can have determined so many contests ...

He fancies his chances so much and that is the difference; he picks up the loaded gun, fires it at his head, laughs as the chamber proves empty and hands the smoking weapon to his opponent to see if he dares pull the trigger.

Really, he cannot bat, or bowl, or field, has hardly taken a wicket or scored a run in proper cricket this season, cricket to which his relationship is roughly that of the music hall to the opera house. He can sweep, clout, nudge, swat and tickle, the unwritten chapters of the coaching manual. He cannot do much with the ball, a little gentle outswing is all. No one is beaten by Reeve, the master of the game, only by Reeve the master of the situation.

>   THE SUNDAY TIMES, August 1994
>   Peter Roebuck on Dermot Reeve

I just hope the stars and planets will be propituously aligned for the young cricketers starting out on their Test careers.

>   TED DEXTER
>   before England v. Australia, 3rd Test, Trent Bridge, 1993

[Ilott] is out of this game with a groin strain and thus joins Darren Gough, Chris Lewis and Andrew Caddick on the list of those more in line for a trip to Lourdes rather than Lord's.
>   MARTIN JOHNSON
>   *The Independent*, 1994
>   Worcs. v. Essex at Worcester

The Cricketer's Quotation Book

BENEDICAMUS

'Praise and bless we famous men …'

R. Kipling

Thank God for Mr. H.P.T.,
Who, with a rare felicity
First shed the floodlight of his mind
On the work-hating, happy hind
That used a sheep-pen for his wicket
And, in the sun, begat our CRICKET.
Thank God for HAMBLEDON'S loved hill
'Neath blue serene or the night wind's will.
Thank God for NYREN, JOHN and DICK,
Of cricket authors JOHN'S the pick,
Though, some aver, he stole a spark
From CHARLIE LAMB or COWDEN CLARKE
Thank God for STEVENS, tight old fella,
And Mrs. LUMPY'S green umbrella,
Thank God for STEVENS, honest LUMP,
Blaspheming us our middle-stump.
Thank God for BELDHAM'S rapier keen,
The BELVEDERE of TILFORD GREEN
Thank God for balls from HARRIS whirling
Like thunderbolts of Jove's own hurling.
Thank God for Mr THOMAS LORD,
Thank God fro Mr WILLIAM WARD,
Thank God for JOHNNY WILLES' stand,
His early fight for overhand.
Thank God for EDGAR WILLSHER, he
Defied the rules of MCC,
And, by his obstinate defiance,

The Cricketer's Quotation Book

Bought, for posterity, compliance.
Thank God for Mr ALFRED MYNN
Sunning his strength by KENTISH inn.
Thank God for FELIX and for BOX,
(And, while he rhymes, for Mr KNOX.)
Thank God for WILLIAM 'LILLY'S' BRACES,
And for his exquisite grimaces,
And for his high staccato shout,
When FULLER PILCH is almost out.
Thank God for Dr WILLIAM GRACE
Who, in his solitary place
Of unassailability,
CRICKET'S RIGHT HAND AND BRAIN AND EYE,
Created BATTING as a SHOW
For rich and poor, for high and low.
Fondly lie that grass upon him
Which undying glory won him.
Thank God for RANJI'S magic glance,
Lord of deft-flickering romance.
For FRY, whose back-stroke came to men
By careful precept, studious pen.
Thank God for JESSOP: Look, he's coming,
All cap-à-peak; the OVAL'S humming;
A catapultine crouch; a crack ...
Where is it? Six: oh, chuck it back.
Thank God for TRUMPER, heavenly blade,
All-daring, more-than-all-repaid.
Thank God for Archie, A.C.M.,
Lancashire's treasure, SYDNEY'S gem.
Thank God for SAMMY, S.M.J.,
Loving and laughing in his play.

The Cricketer's Quotation Book

Thank God for HOBBS, our own J.B.,
Safe in his immortality.
(Thank God – at times – for G.J.V.,
Mouthing superlativity.)
Thank God, no less, for LIONEL TENNYSON,
Bendant, with glower of back-to-wall-menace on.
Thank God for WOOLLEY: no batsman alive
Caresses a cut or persuades a DRIVE
With his secure and Olympian sweep;
The angels in heaven with envy weep,
And, would that DA VINCI might live today
To joy in such other left-handed play.
Thank God for Mr DONALD BRADMAN
Causing some literary madman
To write a weird, seductive letter.
Proving that A or B is better.
Honour to old MARYLEBONE
And its tall Pavilion,
Honour to each grave, green tree
Whispering cricket's history.
Honour to the RIVAL BLUES,
Win or Draw or, d—n it, Lose.
Honour to ETON, Honour to HARROW,
Honour to HENDREN'S particular sparrow.
Honour to brown SURREY'S land
And the half-crown OVAL STAND,
Honour to 'THE COMMONS' dim
Coming or going at sun and mist's whim.
Honour to the VAUXHALL TRAM
And the Surrey LUNCHEON HAM.
Honour to HAYWARD'S MILITARY PICKLE,

The Cricketer's Quotation Book

Honour to all that drives that trickle
Into some far uncharted heaven
While batsmen run the breathless seven.
Honour to the PENNY PRESS
And their slashing fearlessness,
To the thrills with which they lard us,
Honour to our NEVILLE CARDUS
Telling us of English suns
And HORNBY-BARLOW-STOLEN runs,
Regaling our receptive souls
With how good RICHARD TYDDLE bowls.
Honour to CHAPMAN, who, after all, won
SIX TESTS, and lost but a SINGLE GUN.
Honour to YORKSHIRE'S swooping HAWKE
Who doesn't think young men ought to talk,
Honour to Mr VALLANCE JUPP
Who told his LORDSHIP to shut up.
Honour to TRENT BRIDGE and OLD TRAFFORD,
Honour to SYDNEY BARNES and STAFFORD.
Honour to BRADFORD, Honour to LEEDS,
Honour to pitches that nurture weeds;
Honour to all the GREENWOOD men
Who topped the Table once again.
Honour, rich Honour, to that bright FLAME
Which, through the centuries, lights our GAME!
    R.C. ROBERTSON-GLASGOW
    The Cricketer Spring Annual

Sometimes I wonder why I was born in England, where drowsy summers echoed to the sound of leather on wood and the slow march of the seasons was a country idyll marked by progression from one game to the next. I blink my eyes and the hedges are half gone, the lanes poisoned by exhaust fumes, the meadows unending vistas of sprayed corn or laid concrete. But sometimes from a car, or a train window, I see those once-familiar figures in white, standing still and peaceful on mown grass swards waiting for something to happen. It is a tableau that is essentially a part of the summer of my youth.

I don't envy them now, those figures in white with time on their hands; I don't want to take part.

I just don't want them to disappear.

    HAMMOND INNES
    A Straight Bat, 1981

The Cricketer's Quotation Book

It has been said of the unseen army of the dead, on their everlasting march, that when they are passing a rural cricket ground, the Englishman falls out of the ranks for a moment to look over the gate and smile.
J.M. BARRIE

The Cricketer's Quotation Book